People

by
Craig A. Finseth

Firwood Consulting, Inc.
St Paul, Minnesota, US

Firwood Consulting, Inc.
1343 Lafond
St Paul MN US
http://www.firwood.net
inquiries@firwood.net

First Printing, January 2016

Copyright 2016 by Craig A. Finseth.
Images copyright 1998-2015 by Craig A. Finseth.

ISBN 978-0-578-17690-1

Preface

This book is a collection of photographs taken by me over the period 2000 through 2015. It includes those whose main focus is people in some way. In all cases, these photographs were taken as the opportunity arose, and they have not been altered in any way (other than cropping). They are ordered (mostly) chronologically.

When I take pictures like these, I try to take them as a snapshot of a larger story...leaving the viewer to create the story.

Of course, in some cases, they are just people being people.

They are here for you to enjoy. Please do.

May 2002 – House on the Rock, Spring Green, WI

November 2000 – Los Angeles, CA

January 2001 – Las Vegas NV

March 2002 – Minnesota State Zoo, Apple Valley MN

May 2002 – May Day Parade, Minneapolis MN

May 2002 – Friends School Plant Sale, St Paul MN

August 2002 – Bear Island Lake, MN

May 2003 – May Day Parade, Minneapolis MN

June 2003 – Lake Superior Shore, near Lutsen MN

May 2004 – May Day Parade, Minneapolis MN

May 2004 – Canal Park, Duluth MN

August 2006 – Minnesota State Fair, St Paul MN

August 2006 – Minnesota State Fair, St Paul MN

August 2006 – Minnesota State Fair, St Paul MN

September 2006 – Park Point, Duluth MN

March 2007 – Mahtomedi MN

March 2007 – St Paul MN

August 2007 – I-35W Bridge Collapse, Minneapolis MN

August 2007 – Minnesota State Fair, St Paul MN

March 2007 – Dallas Arboretum, Dallas TX

June 2008 – Quartzite Falls Park, Sioux Falls SD

June 2008 – Quartzite Falls Park, Sioux Falls SD

August 2008 – Park Point, Duluth MN

August 2008 – Park Point, Duluth MN

September 2008 – Seven Bridges Road, Duluth MN

October 2008 – Boston MA

June 2010 – St Paul MN

June 2010 – St Paul MN

August 2010 – Minnesota State Fair, St Paul MN

August 2010 – Minnesota State Fair, St Paul MN

August 2010 – Minnesota State Fair, St Paul MN

August 2010 – Minnesota State Fair, St Paul MN

August 2010 – Minnesota State Fair, St Paul MN

August 2011 – Illinois Institute of Technology, Chicago IL (yes, the sign does say "Harlem"...)

April 2012 – banks of the Mississippi River, St Paul MN

April 2012 – Battleship *North Carolina*, Wilmington, NC

April 2012 – Topsail Beach, Ashe Island NC

August 2012 – Canal Park, Duluth MN

May 2013 – Field Museum, Chicago IL

May 2013 – Field Museum, Chicago IL

May 2013 – Field Museum, Chicago IL

May 2013 – Illinois Institute of Technology, Chicago IL

June 2013 – Moose Lake MN

November 2013 – Fort Worth Botanical Garden, Fort Worth TX

November 2013 – Fort Worth Botanical Garden, Fort Worth TX

November 2013 – Fort Worth Botanical Garden, Fort Worth TX

December 2013 – Art Institute of Chicago, Chicago IL

December 2013 – Chicago IL

December 2013 – Chicago IL

December 2013 – Chicago IL

December 2013 – Chicago IL

March 2014 – Washington DC

May 2014 – Enger Tower area, Duluth MN

May 2014 – Canal Park, Duluth MN

June 2014 – Field Museum, Chicago IL

June 2014 – Millennium Park, Chicago IL

June 2014 – Millennium Park, Chicago IL

June 2014 – Millennium Park, Chicago IL

July 2014 – City Plaza Park, Sacramento CA

July 2014 – Sacramento Zoo, Sacramento CA

August 2014 – Como Park Zoo, St Paul MN

August 2014 – Centennial Park, Nashville TN

August 2014 – Centennial Park, Nashville TN

September 2014 – MN Renaissance Fair, Shakopee MN

November 2014 – Royal Ontario Museum, Toronto ON

November 2014 – Royal Ontario Museum, Toronto ON

December 2014 – Christkindlmarket, Chicago IL

February 2015 – Chicago IL

July 2015 – Detroit Zoo, Detroit MI

July 2015 – Detroit Zoo, Detroit MI

July 2015 – Flushing Meadows, Queens NY

July 2015 – Flushing Meadows, Queens NY

July 2015 – Flushing Meadows, Queens NY

October 2015 – Canal Park, Duluth MN

November 2015 – Milwaukee Public Museum, Milwaukee WI